PLUCK
ANOTHER
APPLE,
EVE,
AND
FINISH
IT

PLUCK ANOTHER APPLE, EVE, AND FINISH IT

POEMS BY
HOLLY L. THOMAS

SUN PORTAL PRESS

Published by Sun Portal Press
Clinton, Washington 98236

SunPortalPress.com

Published in the United States of America

ISBN 978-0-9600113-0-8
Library of Congress Control Number:

Cover Photo by Mundusimages via iStock Photo
Cover and Interior Design by Julie Quiring
and Holly L. Thomas

For CJ and my family,
especially my mother, who taught me how to see,
and my father, who taught me how to question.

Contents

Two: Einstein's daughter

Three: Brushwork

Acknowledgments

Versions of several of these poems have appeared in: *Poets Against the War* by Thunder's Mouth Press/The Nation Books (*Chiapas*); The Hawaii Pacific Review (*In the Bamboo, Waiting*); Pontoon Ten (*Healing a Man*); *Tattoos on Cedar* by the Washington Poets Association (*Manna*); Pearl Thirty-Seven (*Blue Back to Blue*); and Floating Bridge Review Number One (*Einstein's Daughter*). *Labradorite* was first published on Shifting the Grid, the blog for sourcingtheway.com.

Halved for the yearling is built from 10-syllable Dekaaz, a form developed by the marvelous Rachel Bagby as a tool for creative facilitation. The syllabic pattern is 2, 3, 5. You can learn more about Dekaaz at rachelbagby.com.

This book has been a long time coming. Of the many friends and allies who encouraged me through many cycles of engagement and retreat, I'd like to thank these people in particular: Joe (CJ) Riley, Noela Hooper, Martha Nicholson, Liz Halverson, Julie Quiring, Laura Strong, Anna Maria Bäck, Jeff Vander Clute, Anne Stadler, Tony Rondolone, Norman David Thomas, Tom Trimbath, Samantha Wilkinson, Doug Flomer, Vicki Robin, Scott Davis, Lana Hechtman Ayers, Suzanne Edson, Fredda Jaffe, Julene Weaver, Vanessa Raymond, Kate Hoch, Tricia Metsker, Linda Hamilton, Mario Juarez,

Doug Kim, Donna and Bill Humphreys, Ken Iwamura, Traci Tabordon, Craig Kerwien, Ellie Matthews, Joannie Stangeland, Annie LaBarge, Sourcing the Way (sourcingtheway.com), the "winter gatherers" at the Whidbey Institute (whidbeyinstitute.org), and the creative community of Whidbey Island.

Finally, to everyone who inspired poems without realizing it, thank you. Something you did made me look, or something you said made me remember.

"We allow for the possibility that reality—all of this universe as we know it—is awake."

Pir Elias Amidon
Seven Contemplations on Awakening

PLUCK
ANOTHER
APPLE,
EVE,
AND
FINISH
IT

One

There must be a word for it in German

Gloria mundi

On this otherwise undistinguished evening,
a man at the garage collects money
in a four-by-five booth
with a rickety heater,
his accented "Thank you"
passed across gloved hands.
A child paws the velour of a pup's ear,
wrestling in an uncoordinated tangle—
hatchlings.
Somewhere off the Kona coast,
porpoises are racing for the hell of it.

Who knows? They could all be God.
Something mightily bare-skinned and brilliant,
as like to us
as the David to the marble
that waited for so long,
hovers in the world.

Pluck another apple, Eve,
and finish it.
We are all promises
watching to see
how we will keep
ourselves.

The loa

*In Voodoo, loas are spirit intermediaries
between people and God. When a loa comes,
whoever it possesses is said to be
"the horse it rides."*

A body is a walkabout for minerals
taking a break from building the world,
to see it. A sentient tube
hosting hordes of purposeful meanderers,
affluent ex-patriots
milling around the stalls of crowded souks.

A buttressed hive of hollow bones
whose guardian cells,
bred to the task of making and destroying,
dispatch troops to herd and feed and cull.

A stardust eddy. A vortexed verb.
A self-organizing braid of flashing densities.

Endocrine instructions pelt the protein sea,
shift the wind,
alter the salt ratio a bit,
tug or nudge the interstitial tide,
and swarm the necessary miraculous,
yes- or no-ing each epigenetic foray
or sudden dare,
presumably unaware of 'me' or 'mind'
as mitochondria churn and burn.

Yet somehow, awareness comes—
the dot of crimson ink in the flask of water.

And it rides that water like a loa.

In the bamboo, waiting

I step off the trail to Hanakapiai Falls
along the green Na Pali
to enter the only bamboo thicket
with a clear way in.

In a cleft between massed trunks
I take two steps, stop
inches from a spider
waiting dead center
in a high-spun web,
its star-shaped carapace
a samurai mask
in ebony, crimson, white.

I breathe across its body.
It won't move.

There are places we can't share
without tearing
what's not ready to be torn.

I back out slowly.

Some traps demand
to be left intact
for their intended.

Rising (Tebenkov Bay)

Through an archway we might glide,
unaware that a distant
instrument
marks our arrival,
measures us excitedly but poorly
like frail pins of a seismograph
set into the wings of a ballet stage
to gauge Stravinsky's genius
by a Firebird's leap.

A meadow of jellyfish
blooms by hundreds
around our kayaks,
colored like peonies
face down, fluttering.
They never break the surface
but stretch it impossibly,
not seeing that we hover
in their sky.

None of us breathe
as they rise.
When we rise,
what stops for a moment
amidst the whirl of measuring
and holds its breath?

Healing a man

My role: Stowaway
orbiting the lip of darkness,
aiming what light I can over
the swallowing curve.

Something kind tethers me
so I won't unwittingly
follow my own prayer
down a throat that knows only
to swallow and crush
all it can.

It seems pointless, this sending light into you
hoping it will return to me encoded and alive,
phosphorescent diatoms
on the breast of a dark sea,
but I persist.

We don't know the limits of possible
so don't speak to me of odds.
Echoes can spring from soft places
and water can re-climb falls,
and light can escape

from the heaviest pull of oblivion
if some number of stars
in some number of galaxies
in some number of dimensions
we may never know
consent
all of an instant
to let it through.
The odds of our being
are infinitely small,

yet here we are.

At the aquarium,
waiting for a wedding to begin

A seahorse in twilight.
Dorsal fin flutters
a soft wave.
Prehensile tail
wrapped around a coral twig
lets go,
curls into the golden ratio
of nautilus,
a perfect Fibonacci spiral.

There was a first time in all time
when something dropped to its knees
in awe.

I speak of that moment
the universe grew into
while its galaxies
spiraled in swept currents,
the first time something
gasped
and knelt
because it didn't know
what else to do.

There must be a word for it in German

Broad and curved as the muscles
of a baker's palm,
this fragment of black glass,
embossed with dots and dashes
like a remnant of some lost bowl
for floating roses in Morse code,

probably fell from a garbage barge,
part of a heap
dumped into midnight water, but I

imagine it whole,
flung from a yacht rail
by a gowned brunette
whose request for rose *water*
the steward didn't understand.

   Before it reached this beach,
   a sea of frictions
   nibbled its edge into scallops
   flaked in small
   concaves

   as if Poseidon,
   moonlighting at a camp
   in the Dakotas
   to practice chipping arrowheads,

swapped salmon for obsidian
and drank obsidian
to make glass out of water.

Something whispers to an archeologist
"This shard suggests an oblong reliquary,
that shard
an amphora for wine,
and this peculiar alabaster detail
is the telltale
of a funeral urn with jackal's head,
not hawk's."

       If arc is to circle as cap is to sphere,
       what is the word for the piece that—
       touched—
       makes inference vault the mind,
       so whoever holds the fragment
       grasps the whole?

If Asia were ever to lift itself away,
the curve of its underside
would mourn the mother sphere.

As for my own continent—
a patch of fur
sashed across the belly
of something restless.

Shattered (lit)

Heat genies rise from the desert.

Around one curve,
another.

Miles in,
the path begins to shine
with fractured light.

A hill, a gleaming path,
a slope ablaze with mica
rises to three mine caves
as small as hermit cells
and empty as a skull's
eye sockets.

I climb to the largest cave,
step from noon into midnight,
and stand inside,
my back to the gouged wall,
eyes closed a long time,
waiting.

I try crouching on pinprick shards,
shadowed,
listening through heat,
but I hear nothing.

A long time still

I stay back in the darkness
waiting.
Nothing comes.

At last
I step to the threshold
and sit in the bright glare.
Every shattered mica chip
scattered on the ground
stares back.

The light is everywhere.
My eyes burn.

Glimpse

I tip a glass over a housefly
exhausted by a night spent
trapped on the wrong side of a window.
I slide a postcard of the Grand Canyon
underneath it,
careful not to crush the creature's legs
against the rim.
I step outside, turn the glass skyward.
The fly flies away.

My heart opens for a moment
as if I were the kind of person
who always frees trapped things.
But I am a fickle god—
unpredictably caring,
intermittently aware,
for the moment, more intrigued
by the odd parallel
between the fly's brief, bewildering
glimpse of the Grand Canyon
and my own brief, bewildering
glimpses of something huge.

Lucy in the sky

"Twinkling in the sky is a diamond star...
50 light-years from the Earth...
[named] after the Beatles song."
David Whitehouse, *BBC News*, 2004

"You'd need a jeweler's loupe
the size of the sun
to grade this diamond."
Imagine all those edges.
Carats in billions of trillions.
The crystallized carbon heart
of a white dwarf,
enough to dazzle every lover
in the cosmos
and facet every face
with diamond eyes.

Every cutting wheel,
every sculptor's saw
and surgeon's knife,
every scribing tool
and driller's bit
could be re-carved
from diamond roughs
as big as ships,
towed across fifty years
of light,
ferried, in pieces,
earthward.

And what say you, Lucy,
of the scalpels of inquiry?
How far into the collective dream
might we penetrate
with such pure material
and so much blade?

Reefs

Life glows anglerfish in black light
spinning up from clouds of krill and plankton
in slow-blues tides.

We are long-finned beauties,
flickers of schooled fish,
mounds of sea stars, shells
and the hermits they shelter,
clownfish and light-spun guppies
hatched from soft round seas.

Great Barrier skin,
by some salt current of mutual agreement,
divides us into colonies—
our ringed corals,
reefs.

After eight days gone

Soil in the clay pots dry

I pour cloudbursts
from a plastic can

false storm

until the lavender
on the balcony
lifts its arms

and the dark-hearted
leaves of cyclamen
chant again

for on the seventh day
they had begun to doubt

One question

Here and there a plover's body,
a cormorant's limp form,
a broken crab, a torn weed
floating.

After asking the sea
one question,
I watch breakers
crash into the headlands.
The late sun's blaze
and wind's edge
burn me cold.

On the wet cliff I listen,
otherwise alone in sinking light,
an irregular lengthening shadow
on worn stone.

This happens too

Scrap the old adage
about closing the barn doors
after the horses leave.
This is the doors blown open
and the stall doors too.
Your horse there, waiting.
This time you can see her wings
but they aren't pretty—
"pretty" wouldn't set you
quaking in your skin like this.

Later,
no matter how much you might protest,
she'll bring you home,
where you'll still need to feed and groom her,
still approach her in muddy boots
with rafts of hay.
You'll still fall asleep on your bed
beside someone or no one,
and wake to the next day, hungry.

If you decide you dreamt it,
she'll nicker as always
for the apple in your pocket,
and welcome your touch,
wings gone.

Theocracy

On a neighbor's roof, a lone crow
walks on invisible feet
through collected rain.

From where I stand, the water's shimmer
hides whatever detritus
the crow is pecking.

All I see is a footless bird
hell-bent on dismembering its reflection.

Whittler

Out on the moon your knife
carves crescent
from disk
to make room
for darkness
that looks
at first
like
nothing.

Throw your own bones

Throw your own bones
into the furrows behind you.
Turn. Watch them rise.
Swallow your pride.
Wave.
Call your own name
to gather them around you.
Walk together
from the jagged ground.

Form a chain of selves
across rivers.
On the far bank
of each impossibility,
grasp your own arms
to clamber up to safety.
Lean against your own breast.
Catch your breath.

Climb through the fields
to the door of the tent
one of you prepared.
Whisper thanks
to the you on watch.
Go in. Lie down.
Rest in the shade
made of your own
shadow.

Sacred geometry

The shortest distance between
two angels is an arc.
Einstein knew.

Backtracking into proof
made his huge brain hum
until there he was,
announcing to all the world
"Space curves."

Between any two points,
as long as gravity is free
to bend it to its will,
space curves.

What if he'd reversed it?
What if he'd said
"Curves space—
the singular path
over a sphere's surface
creates distance?"

Oh, Gabriel and Michael,
take up our balance poles
at the tightrope landings
and feel the rope as we do,

feet chalked for traction,
knees bent for balance and spring.

See how we keep trying
to walk the curve
stretched taut between us,
the shortest way.

Everyday human

We're unknowingly upheld,
water striders
on an infinite surface,
trusting to buoyancy and tension
without looking in
or down.

Labradorite

If I tilt this piece of labradorite just so,
when the angle's right,
the greys of sky and sage
give way to Aurora fire.
Flames beneath the surface
blaze blue-greens
particular to this stone's
particular sheen and qualities.
And also, uncontained, beyond containing,
deep light-lines straight as arrows
cross its face, bridges
to the something more
this piece was part of.

If you acutely angle a mind
in the geometry of surprise
enough to catch its story looking elsewhere,
a soul with the sheen of a rufous throat
and neon-bright, shows itself,
blazing through the story's camouflage,
and all the edgeless lines of light it holds
are pointers to the next soul and the next,
hints of the original urge
to break into so many,
and of the ache for union.

Shattered into everything, the All
reveals its fire through our faces.

The glass

Which way are you—
half empty or half full?
You might argue
there's no question—
just a glass
twice as big as it could be.
Making the glass smaller
is a thought,
but have you ever known a glass,
once taken from the fire
and shaped,
once set aside and cooled,
once put to any use
by any god at all,
to meekly
shrink?

Leave the glass alone awhile
and its implications—
what your answer supposedly
says of you—
entire personality profiles
built on the imagined challenge
of a mute wet vessel.
Leave it alone a week or so,
then look again.
It has been quietly
emptying itself.
There is so much room.

When the morning swimmers turned

Their waterlogged wings thrashed past buoys,
plowing the surface straight toward us,
much too clumsy to rise—
I mistook them for birds
as their capped heads fought the current,
arms curled over and over—
black, wet-suited arms.

The fastest swimmer detoured
a clutch of floats,
chopped rough figure-eights
into the tide churn,
reached the near buoy, stopped.
Others arrived one by one
and huddled,
bobbing like otters resting.

When they resumed swimming,
arm-over-arm still
heavy as oil-soaked wings
compared to the gulls above them,
nothing looked fluid until they turned
parallel to our ferry.
Seen full-length, suddenly sleek as seals,
the long smooth arcs of their arms
with the sun behind them,
they could have been flying.

Each found a rhythm, kicked
a measured but glittering spray
of neither air nor water
but the two combined,
bridging worlds as only we—
stubbornly—bridge them.
From one angle,
how close we seem to foundering
while, from another, we soar.

Goal

On entering
the cave,
to recognize
the den scent
of the Triune
as my own.

One more degree of freedom

When it speaks,
it's not often sound I perceive,
but sensation.
A knife-quick outbreath
concaves my chest;
my heart splits
and refills it.
Tears rise and my mind weighs in
but by then I've already answered.
If I touch a wall to
steady myself,
people who notice may wonder
if something's wrong.
Nothing is wrong.
These are the moments that make me.
The whisper enters;
something breaks open.
One more degree of freedom.
The day goes on.

Spooky action

The man with the thicket eyebrows
was mistaken.
God plays dice with the universe.
God is the love-struck gambler in us all.

Halved for the yearling

As stripe
says to stripe
"I dream of tigers,"
you sleep,
a curtain
billowing open.
You are
what you see.
You see that you are
riding
a planet's
magnanimous mind.
In ten
syllables,
what is your life worth?
Idea
confetti
glitters your free will.
Why not
goose the muse,
fondle your crazy?
Say yes.
Toss apples
halved for the yearling.

The risk

We're the door,
the chamber,
the sleeping in,
the lid on the well,
the water within,
vagrant and bowl,
booth and confessor,
key,
chest,
pirate,
treasure,
the mast, the sail,
the hands, the gale,
the fisher folk,
the fish,
dust come to life,
the curse and the blessing,
the guarantee,
the risk.

World tree

Here's the thing. You spend years, lives,
millennia waking to the news you have a soul.
More years, lives, millennia trying to hear it,
honor it, meet its expectations.

Then something shifts you bigward and you see
your soul is small—small and by now worn—
small and by now worn and by now
burdened—because it has believed you all this
time. It has come to believe in expectations.

It has honored you by trusting your word
through life after life after life. When you
called yourself unworthy of all it offered,
it believed that too and grieved with you.
And with its grief through years, lives,
millennia, every moment knowing what you
felt, it learned shame and fear. Love and joy
as well, yes, but it remembered most
what you kept close.

Here's the thing. Unlike you, who melted back
into the Allness with each death, to be reborn
in new forms convenienced by amnesia, your
soul remembered everything.

Archivist of every self-attack, both child and
bogeyman for every fear, it forgot nothing
except (almost) the innocence you both began

with—the pure curiosity from which the
countless selves of you were created and cast
out—not exiles, though it felt that way,
but seeds.

Here's the thing. You are vaster than your soul
and its long memory, so much vaster that
the 'er' is meaningless.

I speak not to the personal one who goes by
the human name you have this time—not to
that particular amnesiac, however marvelous it
is—and it surely is. I speak to the One from
whom those named selves come. I speak
to your own World Tree.

That tree is vast. That tree is unburdened.
That tree is free of the accumulated weights
your old soul carries, free of its distrusts,
its dreads, its sorrows, utterly, utterly free
of its grave aloneness.

That tree is the Whole of who you are—
both source and record—the original perfection
from which the human you who is hearing this
and all the selves you've ever been were born.

When you realize you are that and look out
from those heights, you see your soul, and the
crust it acquired bravely sheltering your

incarnations shows itself as the trap it has
become and begs for breaking.

Stop asking your soul what it needs as if it's
wiser. From your root and height, as your own
World Tree, know the wiser One you are,
and free your soul.

Standing wu ji

"Standing post"
seemingly so simple,
palms
easy,
spring of the knees
relaxed,
feet
cupping the earth
like warm hands
on breasts.

My spine
a slim young pine,
my chest
hollowed just enough
for shoulders to finally
ease the week
a little.

Arms hold
an invisible
small sun—
this, after all,
is practice—

and every joint readies
to open or close
at a touch,
mimosa frond,

sea anemone,
inward.

My teacher comes,
turns my hands
on their tendon pivots,
moves an elbow
half an inch
or less,
presses the hollow
of my collarbone
to lean me
into my own
breath,

places his hands on the iliac
crest of my hips
and pushes, ever so gently.

"Now" he says.
"Bow from here."

Two

Einstein's daughter

Shrug off the prophet

All you wanted was an easy beer.
Stranger walks through the tavern door
straight to where you're sipping at the bar,
no hello, just looks you in the eyes—

launches into some preamble about
a mountain in Texas waiting
and his will-o'-the-wisp transgressions,
like nettles—no permanent scars,
just lingering alertness
to things that sting.

Eventually, he gets to it.
"A long time ago I followed you.
There were thirteen of us,
not twelve.
Do you remember
who the thirteenth was?"

You say you don't,
trying to shrug off the prophet.
This isn't the first time
a stranger has called you Christ.

And not the Namaste kind,
or the bits we all breathe in
the same way we breathe
molecules of Hitler,
but the nailed kind

with limited time
and a nasty job.

You say you want to
slow your life way down.
The stranger keeps talking.

Of course you understand him.
But if he's right,
you don't want to think about that yet.

Einstein's daughter

Before they wed, their baby
went behind a bolted door,
given into someone else's hands.
After a time, there was no more news.

> Her new parents worried.
> She was nearly three
> but still not speaking.

> At twelve,
> she would sit in the dark
> and stare at the sky for hours.

> At thirty, on a dare,
> she strode into the patent office
> to file an idea too good for its time.

> The clerks who might have guessed—
> her sloped eyes and wild hair—
> were out back, slowly smoking
> their curled pipes.

At fifty, she thought of something
no one had ever heard of
in this world.

Just then, her daughter's toddler
tugged at her hands, crying.
All she remembered later

was that an idea
as miraculous as a bubble's skin
had appeared,
then vanished—

something remarkable,
something she had wanted
to write down.

Innocent

Dangling from a driftwood log
just so,
your feet carve ripples into sand,
kin to the near waves spreading
interference patterns,
ridges of light and dark,
standing waves birthing galaxies.

Your footprints might as well be
doors through the heart of Jesus—
the smallest fragment of fractured silica,
this frail world.

So you stand again as the tide climbs,
staring at the cosmos in a footprint,
wreck the pattern,
ruin some utopia,
mutter a blessing over the unseen.

Understand no thing.
Walk the waterline borderless
and empty.
Stones with stories you can't imagine
growl underfoot.
Tears surge with grief, awe, and recognition,
and each tear regresses
back to the limitless this:

Today

you believe the Origin is wakeful
and that all of this—
light darkness, crushed utopias—
all petitions one heart to another,
all songs, all waters,
all imaginings, all fears,

all exist because
something somewhere
once grew curious.
Some maddeningly vast
Innocent
asked
"What if….?"

The first weaver

The Mexican hoisted parrot colors
to his shoulders,
cotton blankets
as bright as sky and peppers—
chili red, snake-eye yellow,
Curaçao turquoise—
and spread them on the beach
at Sayulita.

I hardly haggled.
He wanted so little for this one
spun from seed tufts
plucked from barbed plants,
harvest of pricked fingers
and bent backs.

Look back years in thousands.
Stroke seed silk.
Dream spun thread.
Weave of thread and fingers
that first strip.

Build a frame of rope-strands
tied to willing greenwood
strung and braced
to weave a wider cloth.

Scrape vine, boil indigo,
collect annatto and cochineal.

Drench the sleeping cotton yarn
with color.

My hands travel this blanket
of their own accord,
remembering something I don't—
plants that whispered,
those first hands
that listened.

Manna

"Let no man leave any of it till the morning...
And the people of Israel ate the manna forty
years, till they came to a habitable land."
Exodus 16

As we slept a dry crust fell,
shimmering star grounds or moon crumbs
dusted our tent cloths
and the rock grit
that roughened the desert.

It fell equally on the backs of sheep
and the eyelids of shepherds.
It fell and waited.

We had gone to bed hungry,
homesick for Pharaoh's slave halls.
We woke to find manna
scattered like desert dust
everywhere.

That was the first morning God rained food,
years before we knew we would eat this
forever,
before summoning water from rock
kept us from dying,
before the commandments boomed
over the mountain,
before Moses smashed the idol,

before the calf-gold became the ark.
Manna still falls.

> I once met a slave from the East
> who spoke of snow—cold white
> powder
> that smothered the mountains
> he'd fled to—
> stiff white water that dazzled
> the winter peaks.

> It could comfort and kill.
> He nearly died from its splendor.
> Shifty as dunes,
> it deepened
> day after day,
> crept forward,
> receded,
> blinded,
> sheltered,
> buried.

> He survived
> but was captured and sold into Egypt.
> Others he loved stayed in it
> and disappeared.

But this—this manna from God—
was something different,
"like coriander seed, white,
and the taste of it
like wafers made with honey."

We had one chance
to eat of it each morning.
Whatever we held for later
spoiled by noon.
We learned quickly
to trust
and to worry.
No amount of hoarding
would feed us
if God forgot.

Chiapas, 2002

I don't know you, child.
I've never seen your country
or spoken your tongue.
But I see you burning
like an oil-soaked rag
in one of the old farm trucks
torched to terrify your people,
burning alone
because you fell asleep
after a long day's bending
in stone fields,
too tired at day's end
to walk back home.
Or...because you were
dragged there
conscious, and
set aflame.

Your mother devours your murderers' hearts
in her drugged dreams.
Your father, 'disappeared' after the burning,
eats his own.

The beckoner

Full-throated at nightfall,
his hands cup his mouth
to amplify his voice
and send it.

The same hands once raised
a healed owl to the air,
lifted it together and,
swiftly parting,
left the owl to choose
between flight and falling.

The beckoner calls lost souls.
Hearing his voice,
they choose—
toward
or away.

Hiding

In a shuttered attic, behind
the stack of inherited scrapbooks
lettered in unremembered hands,
hidden by listless gowns
in yellowed plastic,
some brittle version
of an unlived dream grows
bone by bone.

No more than a rib cage
so far,
but each year adding,
hardening,
fleshing itself in cobwebs
for lack of skin and sinew,

it makes what it can
from neglect—
vertebrae, a skull—until
whatever your dream becomes
if all it's ever fed
is dust and darkness
stirs
and starts
creeping
toward
the stairs.

A hapless waxwing

Tall in gathered silk,
still as a waiting heron,
she watched the antique pendulum arc
and breathed in the gardenias.

She would accept his proposition—
embrace the anaconda to keep warm.

A hapless waxwing fluttered
at the skylight.
Down on the terrazzo,
a single gendarme danced.

Above tree line

On this slammed-down knuckle
of a mountain, boulders
heaped beyond careening
wait and watch.
Pockets of their lichen coats
bulge with durable mysteries,
fractured histories,
rumblings from angles of repose,
tales of how time
spins and spills and tumbles
as it flattens, tilts, and splits
jagged lines of fault
with veins of precious heresies.

Ancestor

Her hands curled into shells
around her ears
to gather all the muttering.

They decided a particular rustle
was fawn foot
or grouse wing
or wind spurt
kicking the scent of pine thatch
back to the high trees.

She might have known
how to mark each sound
in inflected lines
scratched in bark
or stone,

but I've no chisel trace,
no rune,
no glyph for fur
or fragrance,

no sign of what
her ears spent years
inscribing.

Climb

Lone heart,

lean
into the thermal.

Catch
the spiraling current's
reach.

Leap to its heat
from your nest
of fitful
preparing.

Ride the invisible column
of pillowing air.
Rise
now
from your aerie

lest your talons stiffen
and your wings
fail.

Climb
now.
For a moment comes

when the air cools

and you,

exposed as a fledgling
despite
your years,
must
beat your wings
with all your blessed strength
to make your own way skyward
or,
hesitant,
fall.

Tulipa

I am tight flush red,
a bud on a straw
cut from the mother bulb,
feeling for water.

My petals carve
a red blaze
down to a jet-black
cup,

each petal tipping
its own dark
triangle of attachment.

This is my first spring.
I have forgotten all others
but I know what I am.

Lace at the boudoir window
reveals what it conceals.
Suspended
in this slim vase
my long neck is beauty,
my cupped sex.
I start to open in the morning light,
a bride.

Days in the cool air of propriety
I open to morning,

close to night.

A little boost of heat
or fear
and my petals spread wide,
split like an acrobat.

I   hesitate
to shut myself tonight.
I won't   can't
close my petals—
splayed limbs stiff from posing,
losing color.
Too soon
blousy as a harlot's housedress.
Slipping.

My anthers throb
on their silk filaments.
My ovary aches.
Time spins. Bee beyond the glass—
come in!
I'll take all comers now.

Even though I know
I can't make
anything,
everything I'm made of
is for making.

Relic

The ten-foot curve of whale jaw
hauled from a salt coast snarl
waits to be hung high
in the stripped fir rafters.

You run your hands over
the bleached bone, relic
of the whale's last breach.

How many times
had its belly smacked water
and its fluke slipped down
before it came to this,
its beached hulk broken,
claimed and scavenged clean?

Far from the driftwood catacombs
where you found it
on your knees,
plunderer and pilgrim,
the bone claims sanctuary,
promises sanctuary,
under your roof
upheld by old bone trees.

Under Greenland ice

Meltwater tunneling down from ice sheets
lubricates underlying bedrock, hastening the
slippage and break-up of ancient ice.

I, who have
no memory
of anything
but stillness,
have started
to hear
rumblings,
mycelial
whispers
of something
after
and something
other than
this weight,
something
different from
this holding
so much cold.

I am rock down deep.
What's above me
isn't what's below.

That's all I've known
for so long,

it's been
everything.
But something
strange
is touching my
scarred surface,
looking
for quick ways
across and through,
bringing sounds
that summon
recollections.

II

I speak only rock.
Rock speaks slowly.
Water—now I remember—
water hurries.
Water finds hurry, makes hurry,
makes more hurry sliding
over rock.
I am still still,
but where water wants to go,
it goes.
I know the weight
of the ice sheet's mass
above me,
but this new wetness
touching my face
is melting space

between me and that ice.
And besides the water's chatter,
sometimes there's a sharp sound.
Cracking.

III

I've remembered
water's language.
I'm still rock.
The ice has thinned
and I've begun to rise.
There's a brightening blue
where blackness was.
I had forgotten light.
Soon, by my reckoning,
soon in a season
like all the seasons
since the water found me,
the last of the ice will melt,
or crack, or,
like so much of the rest of it,
slide away.
The water, too, will leave
as I rise up.
For the first time
since eons before this,
my remembering,
began,
I'll meet the sky.

A boy at the river mouth

The girl by the quay
waits for the ocean
to kiss her knees,
soak her skirt cloth,
wet her sapling waist.

The boy at the river mouth
balances cobbles
sorted by flood tides,
watches the tide surge inland,
watches the waters
rise to lift one girl.

Runner

Centered in the breastbone,
woman surging forward
alongside traffic at day's end,
darkened street,
pattern of footfalls
soft and steady.

Strip the rest away—
rhythm, body, sound,
thought machine
keeping balanced motion.
All that's left
is an unearthly trace
of light quickly passing
over sacred ground.

Morels

Each swollen shaft
and furrowed hood
thrust from the earth,
filled with the random hope
of coming in a seeker's hand,
yields to fingers skilled
in gathering essence,
the musky sweet reward
for stroking Pan.

Before the separation

You start climbing the wet ladder.
He swims up from behind, rises
halfway from the midnight lake,
stops you.
His fingers
work below the water line.
You sway and
without a word
step down,
half floating,
half exposed
to the August night,
wet breasts shining
with the half-lit moon.
You turn toward him,
balancing
with one arm
on the ladder.

The water toils and churns
and waves roll out in all directions,
as if some great beast
were at the surface,
struggling.

From the south rim

Eventually this too will wear away
through epochs' worth of weather
and persistence,
despite the desert zones
and stones' resistance.
How imperceptibly the change begins.
As long as the water keeps moving,
it always wins.

Beethoven's nude

She leans back,
an upright Odalisque
on a paint-scuffed stool,
neck arched for the opulent curve.

The instructor nods—
plenty to keep them busy—
twenty minutes on the timer,
locks it in.

Beethoven's Appassionata
drifts across her skin.
Notes on currents
of heated air
float across
scratched charcoal.

The students try to capture her on paper.
She listens and can't help smiling,
each breath an irresistible crescendo,
the smile a glissade across her lips.

What if he were to see her this way—
still as silence,
naked as any woman,
ringed by leggy easels
and insistent eyes,
but listening?
Heaters hum, fluorescent lights

buzz her heights and shadows.

Beethoven's sonata soars from a small disk
spinning in a plastic box.

Of this whole scene, her womanly shape
is all he'd recognize.

Deaf, he wouldn't even know why
she was smiling.

Taos

Over land
pregnant with ochre

there
in the high sky

color
almost-muskmelon

slashed cavity

wet
with seeds
of thunder.

Three

Brushwork

Only

Here we are again in this life, edging closer,
skittish as wild dogs near camp light,
destined to someday kinship across
split kingdoms.

I try to remember how to fill
and empty the same heart,
but there is no how.

Like the you I imagine,
I am so human here,
and there is only
only.

Star island, 1967

The island shaped each limb,
saved each feature,
covered my mouth with amber
to preserve it.
When I left for the last time,
pine roots kissed my feet.
Deer moss blessed my skin
to keep it tender.
Water drank my voice.
Thunder-scented cedar
stroked my hair.

All that I knew there
I still know,
but forget I must remember.

I learned what goodbye means there,
but I take it back.

Now my grown face
masks the younger,
bare and weather-worn,
each line a pine root
probing island rock,
my eyes
clearings the island
passes through.

Wolf

Near my shoulder she pants like a renegade
accustomed to long runs
and hard stops.
Prescient.
Familiar.
Mine.

Once, when I was young and lost,
I thought a predator stalked me
in bleak country.
I foundered, a doe in a quagmire,
a buck in thorns,
bent double by slashes of heartbreak.
I wrenched my legs from the muck
and lurched forward,
raw and shaking.
Fear kept me moving—
fear of what might happen
if it caught me.

That is how she led me home
the first time.

Magical thinking

In the mirror time
a piece of self
comes back.
How young she is.
How hesitant.
Exile thin.
Certain all that happens
is her doing,
a caged pigeon
trained in superstition,
sure that hopping clockwise
makes its food appear.

Problem is
she claims more blame
than credit.
She won't understand
what I've become,
but a seat at the table of memory,
I can give her.
At least,
with the other prodigals,
she'll be fed.

Not yet prophecy

Onshore lights
ribbon
the black water.
Waving
columns of photons
masquerading
as lit poplars
spark
rippling leaves
with fire.
You are somewhere
beside the sea
or thinking of it.
Tunneling
the for side of ever,
this unsteady
brilliance
across black water
is my first glimpse
of you
surfacing.

Petal

my fingertip against the rose petal

somewhere in the chasm of two skins
imprecise exactness

rose tip against me

space between thought and presence
cuts bindings that won't be bound

unties its own
incurved
scented intimacies

unfurls unity
beyond the horizon of capture

"We have not come to take prisoners"

Title from Hafiz
as translated by Daniel Ladinsky

You're already
in me,
a new taste
spreading suddenly
over my tongue,
filling my mouth
before I can even
name you,
a bittersweet
so startling,
instead of swallowing,
I gasp.

What I fill

Paint puddles viscous with laziness
wait as if I'd lifted them from tar pits,
beasts turned into multi-colored sludge,
witless, reluctant to stir.

I tickle them with water,
supple them with thinner,
flatter them with promises of fame.

They fall for it.
Alizarin crimson takes cobalt's measure.
Cadmium yellow is at the ropes,
on edge.
Phthalo blue flexes a thigh, sends
red ochre flying.
Brushes drip paint on the carpet.
I didn't plan this. I'm too impatient
to fetch a cloth, to lay out
protective gear, to stop daring the colors to
surprise me.

Splashes of bottle-blue spatter the edges
with shapes that are nothing but color
until
a ribbon of characters
rises from each finger,
like startled spirits of the freshly dead
yanked from
the whiteness they expected

toward this borealis flare.

Paint flecks wet, skin busy,
my fingers travel my body
and opt at a moment's notice
to enter its darkness—
to see if three primary colors
as promised
blend to black.
What I fill,
I empty.
Fingertips more sensitive
than any brush, I am
distracted
by a glimpse of myself
shaking.

Look out from the inn

Windows at the Edgewater
split the air.

Up too early, I watch rain
slip into seawater below me
while the window sweats.

A jellyfish floats up.
Its tentacled death cap
flattens and swells,
almost breaks the surface,
sinks away.

Between us, a cold-water wind
scatters sine waves.
Rain tracing rings within rings
leaves honeycomb prints.

And the window itself—
a tricked fluid temporarily upheld,
destined to sink from its own
weight, given time.

I breathe, in my own way floating,
lungs as spongy as nested tentacles,
blood as salted with sea brine
as the slow-sinking Medusa.

In my fiftieth year

In my fiftieth year I seem to be going quiet.
Friends ask what's happening.
My answers are fewer than they
used to be,
saving themselves
like secrets to share later.

Winter storm outside my window
tosses the boughs of the hill cypress
like feathers. Gulls
skitter past on drunkards' wings.
I kiss my own hands
and press them to the glass.
I sit, finally, and listen to Whatever.

Not to be grim—
a family tendency toward grimness
having shown itself already—
my heart has felt enough shattering to know
mending is her birthright—
a boxer's nose,
scarred by personal history,
irreparably dented by connection.

Given the ring we are all born into
no blow is surprising, but still,
I am surprised.

Despite—perhaps because of—that

she sings like a half-wrecked beauty
with no mirror to discourage her,
gardening in daylight,
still gardening at dusk.

I am old enough to know that those
who say there are no mistakes
are themselves mistaken.

But at last
in the war against my self
I have found the good sense to surrender.
And, oh blessed conqueror,
my first word to my disheveled captive
must be, as promised, *freedom*.

Enso (a love poem)

That day

my skin

was rice paper

drinking
from a bamboo
brush

that bowed
to the waiting
blankness

and knew
exactly
how
to pray

a circle.

Fever

This year
the urgent season
brings no one.
You still ache
inside me.

So I cup my hands
under sea stones.
Their curves
fill my palms
imperfectly
and I ask if
licking the salt
from these
granite pebbles
is what's left?

Even if it's sunset and I'm naked standing
face toward the ocean,
my hands overflowing with pebbles,
is this all?

The spotted leopard in my heart
is pacing.
Hungry, impatient, it remembers climbing a
tree
it's never seen,
where its tail twitched while its eyes
raked the plains

looking for the bright flash of life.
It knows the savannahs of more—
wild acacias and grasses
born to be lost in.
These stones in my hands don't quiver
the raw business of life
and I crave life.

If I look to the caged one pacing
I must free it,

for if it can't stalk its prey
of blazing sky and heat,
of scent and fur and movement and yes! union
and crazed joy! through this earth's grim reason
and sweet hope,

my neck
will have to bend to the great beast's hunger,
and into its jaws
I will disappear.

Circling

Paired, we circle the updraft.
Spread-feathered,
poised,
eyeing each other,

we balance the air,

keeping a distance
between us.

In falling meadows
below us,

field mice emerge
from their burrows
and rabbits graze.

Still we climb,
taking our rest
from hunting.

We climb,
intent on soaring,

distracted by air.

Burrs

After *Concerning the Atoms
of the Soul*
by John Glenday

You seem to be arriving sideways,
impression of motion,
hint of spin,
but gently,
doucement, doucement,
to befriend
this seeker of quiet.

I need to drift to earth again
and stay here—
ash from perennial fire—

and I'm more likely to
if you land first,
if you find surface and shelter,

but nothing in this is passive.
Gravity is an act of falling. We leap out—
not down—
none of us ever sure
which world gathered us last time
or will gather us next.

Who am I to fall toward you?
If we are perfect spheres of soul

slipping down
through layer after layer
toward some impossible
center,
our bodies are burrs,

snags in ragged coats
grabbing passing furs
with ingenious hooks,

barbed fruit,
ultimate friction,

determined
to get somewhere
and open.

There, in the woods

Before dawn while I waited by the road,
a movement in the black woods caught my eye.
A sliver of light hung from a tree
deep in the outstretched arms
of broad-shouldered hardwoods.
It held the far beam of a porch lamp
and danced with a flickered rhythm,
heedless and eerie.

I thought it was a wayward strip of something,
a fragment of a warning strung on wire,
a glittered semaphore,
a boundary mark.
It might as well have been
some shimmering scrap
ripped from an elvish hem.

Last night you told me
you are getting stronger.
You said your will
is tempering like steel.

What if this glimmer shone
from your new armor?
What if the light in the woods
was your new skin?

Come back

Teasing a long parched spell,
mist heavy with almost
visits my balcony
one shy hour,
smells of silk,
tastes green.

Its drifts
nearly coalesce into
something
but,
more the phantom of rain
than rain itself,

they moisten the lips of roses
in the downstairs beds
but offer the soil nothing.
They can't gather enough
to give enough
to pool and ripple the dips
in the city's roofs.

Parched sedge-plumes on the ledge,
backlit by bleached feather grass,
bow to their own soil
in baked clay.

I too taste one droplet at a time—
whatever happens to fall

on face or fingers.
Too long I have missed you
like the sedge
her rain.

Each a paper wing

Yesterday, walking the bay road,
I lifted a hemlock branchlet
from the pavement—
freshly broken, dazzled with cones,
each its own spiraling complexity.

I carried it home,
held between my palms
like a stunned bird
waiting to recover.

This morning in my kitchen
it showered seeds, each a paper wing
filled with whatever seeds need
to wed rain to light,
stuffed like a kerchief on a hobo's stick,
essentials to start
the experience of experience
in soil moist and deep enough
on the lee side of somewhere.

My yard has no such soil.
Still, as if I were guiltless,
I step outside and scatter the seeds
from the *carpe diem*
of my hands.

Meniscus

I glide on the meniscus of the heart,
making a slight impression,
worried a little about whether I'll sink
if somehow I clumsily pierce it.

I mimic the beautiful swimmers beneath me
as carefully as I can, as if I
were swimming in their world.
I want these beings
who breathe in love without drowning
to see me here.

Could such swimmers
envy me my freedom?
If they suddenly swam for the surface
and reached up for my hands,
would it be to pull me in
or to climb out?

Myrtle

My father took my picture in the Rockies.
I was twelve, smooth skinned, reedy,
walking in a field of crimson paintbrush.
He asked me to pose for a moment
where my hands feathered the flowers.

My mother, the artist, surveyed the scene
like a painting. The paintbrush blossoms
matched my summer sweater.

He photographed her at fifty.
Somewhere in Yellowstone she leaned
into a high slope
milky with bear grass,
her polio hand half-hidden
by the stronger,
her eyes on the camera,
her smile, as always, shy.
She and the sky were wearing
the same turquoise.

On this Cascade slope
I take the meadow path.
Below the snowfield, paintbrush
crowds blue lupine.
A lone stalk of bear grass
stops me in mid-memory.
It's round, proud, full, pliant,
ready to suckle the sky.

A sign says Myrtle Falls waits farther on.
I almost walk past without seeing the name—
my mother's—
but I reach the falls and linger,
and of all the things to think,
I think of this:

When she was a girl
her father told her
her name meant nothing.
Myrtle was sacred to Aphrodite
and Demeter.
Garlands of myrtle meant triumph,
honor, love.
She knew the myths, but
my mother believed her father.
Now she's here in bear grass
and mountain water.
What is it to miss
the blessing in a name?

Some kind of explanation

You are spun now
into the great threads,
cloth woven of galaxies' dust,
charged bits of light–matter
borne on solar winds.

You are suspended in dew on new webs
strung from branches dripping with catkins,
high-faced and perfectly ordered,
and you glisten, stretched from tree to tree
above night-born paths.

You are cells in my hands
building skin and sinew,
cells dying
and cells replaced,
each with a part
in teaching me
to reach,
and shape,
and hold.

Twenties (Ithaca)

We climb to the falls past misted stone,
tuned to the old creek's salutation.
The Gorge favors shade-lit, sturdy lives.
Violets open. Birches glisten.
Catkins, columbines, morels seduce
while the rock walls listen.
Water keeps hurtling over the cliffs,
and survives.

From as far as I can go

I call to you today
through a gray seal's mouth,
smoothed and soothed
in the throat of a traveling sea,

and through this empty shell,
white with a rose translucence,
plucked from the seamless beach
the seal is watching.

Blue back to blue

No one saw me toss it
from the chopper's window.
That coral you gave me
to take to Alaska
rests in its blue grave,
a crevasse
in a shrinking glacier
near Valdez.

I couldn't have found
a more alien place
for that skeletal piece
of your dive
in a southern sea.
The blue of the ice,
bold as the vivid blue
of a Virgin quay.

Glaciers recede.
Someday the coral piece
will be released
if it isn't ground to silt.
Some future hiker may
lift it all, intact,
from the glacial milk,
or a kayaker may
unknowingly raise dust coral
to the sun
with a paddle's turning.

I brought your coral north.
You carried my poem under,
left it bottled near the stern
of a sunken wreck, pressed
down by a hundred feet
of shifting water.
No one saw you do it.
It's unlikely ever to be found.

Virgin

In the kitchen, I peel pears
from a backyard tree
to add to the apples
in my sauce pot—
the peeler,
plain like my mother's
and her mother's,
fool-proof.

Done separating heaps of apples
from their tight skins,
I've slipped back
from a daydream
because the pears
feel different.
They moisten
under the blade.
They slip free of their skins
instead of clinging.

My hand glides
bottom to tip,
over and over,
peeling each pear
as if stroking
the buttocks' curves.

Tell me there are virgins yet
who are so in love,

so willing,
and so unabashedly sprung
from the women of their line,
that when they first make love
they taste of everything.

Nightly,
some new woman
lets the last veil fall.
Curves,
the far meridians
of her body's
love,
laid bare.

Sleeves don't reach my wrists

This Christmas morning, I sip tea,
wearing the past
like an old chenille robe,
too familiar to part with
but ill-fitting.

The sleeves don't reach my wrists
the way they used to.

My arms keep growing.

Attention

Arresting my tumble back from nowhere

this
hummingbird's hoverflight
          quick-flicking-fingernail alarm
deep-bass-fly-by buzz   *this*

          greenfire wing   *this* bronze blurrrrr
cast emeralds

          this feathered huzzah!

          impossible motion   impossible *flight*

this instant HERE

this instant

gone

Brushwork

My mother told a story
of a Chinese painter
who agreed to complete a landscape
in forty days.

He disappeared into the mountains
with no brushes or scrolls.

On the fortieth morning
he returned to his patron's home
and took up his tools.
By dusk the painting was finished.

The patron grumbled
"I won't pay you for forty days
when you've hardly worked one.
I refuse to pay."

The painter rolled up the scroll
and prepared to leave.

On the threshold he touched his head
and then his heart.
"For forty days I have painted
here and here.
Forty days.
Forty years preparing."

Wind prayer

Blessed wind,
blow me in toward shelter.
Bend me far as the aspen bends
or shake me free
as spent leaves in October.
Hasten my ripening.
Quicken my strengthening.
Show me the worth
of deep roots and suppleness.
Help me learn
to balance the tumult
that living in free air chances.
Give me the gift of stillness
now and then.

Color it sky blue

I sit in the Queen Anne Starbucks near
two women who are talking on their phones—
the nearest one, perhaps in her twenties,
apparently to a sibling arranging care
for one of their parents.
Words about which of them can stop
at Target tomorrow for a few essentials,
and who can shift their schedule a bit
to make room for some task or errand
for the ones they love.
It sounds like this is an ongoing,
not a one-time thing.
The look on her face
when I glance her way
hints so.

She's young for a caregiver,
young to have a voice so
deep and round with responsibility,
but her voice is clear.
At the end, when she says "thank you"
to whoever is on the receiving end of the call,
it's with her heart,
and when she adds "I love you,"
something comes into being in the room.

Within a few seconds the second woman,
seated at the table behind her,
on a quick call to someone,

also says "thank you,"
also with her heart. Her face relaxes.
When she ends her call and turns
back to her computer,
I swear I can feel the first woman's
"thank you" reach
for the second woman's "thank you"
like a hand, extended.

Seconds later, an elderly woman
comes in, looking for something,
and asks a question of a fourth woman,
a teenager seated near the door.
All I can hear is the end of their exchange
when the elderly woman leans toward the girl
to say "thank you so much"
in the way of one who means it—
as if she'd opened an unexpected small
and perfect gift.

You know how it sounds when the words
have the resonance of our blood behind them,
the strength of connections weaving,
and you know the shine they can leave behind,
as if every true "thank you" and "I love you"
were a smattering of gold dust
around a footprint.

The first two women's thank you's
reach out to the elderly woman's thank you,
and when the teenager,

who's apparently already doing
whatever favor was asked of her,
adds "really, it's no problem at all,"
with that offhand sincerity that's both
well-mannered and true,
something in the air lights up between them
and reaches all the way to me
and to the big man in the Seahawks jersey
who's typing at the table beside mine,
and to the windows shining out
onto the avenue,
and to the sidewalk,
and to everyone in range,
like a flicker of lit music.

And I wonder, if I could see a map
of all the thank you's and I love you's
offered and received
in all our human languages
in one day,
what would it look like?
All those short links between people
standing with or near each other,
and all those longer links stretched
across distances.

And if you mapped all the thank you's
and I love you's
for all the days that human beings
have ever lived,
and made the map for each day a still image,

and connected all those images into a film,
what kinds of patterns and tides
would the film reveal?

In that moment I realize that if, when I am
dying, I could see a map
of all the thank you's and I love you's
I gave and was given in this life,
that map would show me
what I had accomplished here this time.

I hear "color it blue, that map—
color it sky blue."
I silently say "yes" and instantly
the idea of the image comes to rest.
Its energy shifts, completed,
as if, by my having had these thoughts,
somewhere such a map has been created,
so from now on I can try to picture it,
and for the rest of my days in this life,
help it grow.

Esperanto

Weeks ago, the hilltop's cherries
surrendered their blossoms
to gutters and walks
and buttoned themselves
into more sensible greens,
but here's a tree with one
brand new pink ruffle,
startling among
thousands of dark leaves,
a petticoated marvel
in peak bloom,
spectacularly late,
all the more vivid for it.

Forced to choose,
I'd take wonder
over understanding.
Tempted to pluck and keep it,
I leave the blossom there,
a scented love note in Esperanto,
the universal language I don't speak.

Trinity

I need to come back from ideas sometimes
and sit,
when the geometry
seems more abstract to me
than sacred,
when believing we co-create all this
seems too much or nothing,
when the responsibility is too heavy
despite sharing it with everything
across within beyond all time and space.

When the veil thickens and turns opaque,
when parts of the tender human I am
hurt,
when I'm unsure, afraid, or sad
(most often sad),
I need something like me to sit with me—
someone, I mean,
not consciousness,
not gods.

So today I imagined sitting
with Mary Magdalene
and her famous husband,
the three of us cross-legged in a triangle,
knee to knee.

Jeshua held my left hand, Mary my right,
and they held each other's.

We leaned in so our foreheads almost touched.
I imagined Jeshua's sun-browned arms,
his robe, his hands,
Mary's arms, my hand in hers,
our silence,
I at first as a child,
their child,
then as the woman I am.

I prayed to them and with them,
asked them to stay close,
said I need them to be this way
sometimes—
whatever they are now,
whatever they were then.

I wept—of course I wept—
and breathed, and eased,
imagining our heads bowed
in simple stillness.
My heart gentled itself
and rested.
My thoughts slowed.

I know this was me
conjuring from longing.
But whatever trapped hurt
had made me cry out
went free.
I can't comprehend infinity,
divinity, or timelessness,

the consequences of entanglement,
or now,
but these two beings
who know what it is to be human—
these two infinities
who help me trust my life—
these two companions
steady, stir, and still me.
This trinity—
this trinity
is mine.

72536732R00085

Made in the
USA
Middletown, DE